Jumping - S

Poems

Leo Aylen

For Trevor
with best wishes
Leo Aylen
7. 11. 85

Sidgwick & Jackson
London

good to meet you
at lunch.

By the same author

POETRY
(published by Sidgwick & Jackson)

I, Odysseus (1971)
Sunflower (1976; 2nd imprint 1979; 3rd imprint 1982)
Return to Zululand (1980; 2nd imprint 1980; 3rd imprint 1982)
Red Alert: this is a god warning (1981)

also
Discontinued Design (Venture Press 1969)

CHILDREN'S OPERA

The Apples of Youth (Chappell & Co. 1980)
(Music by Annette Battam)

CRITICISM

Greek Tragedy and the Modern World (Methuen 1964)

TRAVEL

Greece for Everyone (Sidgwick & Jackson 1976)

First Published in Great Britain in 1983
by Sidgwick & Jackson Limited
Copyright © Leo Aylen 1983
ISBN 0 283 99031 7

Printed in Great Britain by
Needham Printers Limited,
London EC2A 4BA
for Sidgwick & Jackson Limited
1 Tavistock Chambers, Bloomsbury Way
London WC1A 2SG

Contents

A house in Brixton 1
Ten years after the sale of his
trucking business 2
The piano-playing tramp 4
The wood-carving sailor 5
The case of the sunrise
spraygunner 6
Surbiton Harry 7
Chocolate-box blonde 8
Miss Elsie Fitchett 8
The hole 9
A man with dandruff in a
tube train: Sonnet 10
Flop 11
Paradise Lost, according to
Jimmy Rootback 11
Canterbury Bell love-song 12
Blow-dry 13
The two lovers on separate sides
of an impending civil war 14
Nootka princess 14
Island love-song 15
Upside-down song 15
The teddy-bear cobras 16
At the deathbed of the nun who
broke her vows 17
Lake-lady 18
The green god's touch 18
Light from a stone 19
After Wordsworth's *"I travelled
among unknown men"* 20
Imitation of Fitzgerald's *Rubaiyat* 21
The first portrait 22
Thumbnail song 23
The tree of second sight 24
When I am king 24
I held the song in my hands 25

Old age make-up 26
Death of a dancer 27
Test result 28
Now, only the fire can tell 28
Industrial accident 29
Holiday death 30
Attempted escape 32
Murder by hypnosis 32
No reprieve 33
Mystic or schizophrenic 34
Filling our bodies with space 34
In the consulting room 35
Breakdown story 36
Suicide at a board meeting in
a hotel room 37
Massage for back-pain treated
as a yoga exercise 38
Peace the conqueror: Vilanelle 39
Acceptable print 40
The defocussing process 41
Many are called, but few
are chosen 42
The sixteenth vision 43
The peace-piece joker 44
The journey is inwards 45
No "Heaven-Haven" 45
Shadow on the spine 46
The pain-gift 47
The mystic 48
Eucharist: Vilanelle 50
The lame saint 51
Christmas Eve 52

Occasional Verse
Soul of a nation 54
Poet Bloodknot 56
Epilogue to a Diverting Spectacle 58

for Evan and Puck

"Up, valiant soul, put on thy jumping-shoes
Of love and understanding."

Meister Eckhart, as quoted by Andrew Young
in *A Traveller in Time*

Soul of a Nation was commissioned by the BBC for the film of that name, first transmitted in January 1980, with the narration spoken by Sir John Gielgud.

The author wishes to thank Stephen du Sautoy for his help in selecting and editing this collection, and Peter Southwell-Sander for his help in preparing the manuscript for publication.

Jumping-Shoes has been sponsored by Needham Printers Limited with an interest-free loan of the production cost.

A house in Brixton

Street lined, not with gold, but with hub-caps, rubble,
Windscreen shatter, plastic wrappings,
Burn-butts, coughs of wino spittle,
Barbed-wire strands, vest-fragments flapping,

And one door: blue with a stucco arch
Of flowers picked out — rose, white and green;
Flower-frill curtains, parrot on a perch,
Flowering shrub, step spick-an'-span clean.

Every morning the limping widow,
After dreams of her birthplace's tropical sand
Tide-surfed whiter than Persil, steadies
Herself on her steps, the broom in her hand

Her black-power-fist-flag of liberation,
Which sweeps the Mother Country's droppings
Of half-eaten ice-cream and chips, dog faeces
And bottle-smash up to the passport office

Of her own dustbins, till a new lot of roughs
Rip them and repatriate the rubbish
On her bright doorstep whose flowers insult
Their homo-sap trash with her monkey scrubbing.

"Why do you do the Council's job?"
"Why bother about other people's filth?"
Her unconscious answer of brush and mop
Flaunts at the master-race her wealth

Of birth by a palm-framed fish-wriggling shore
Where a girl that was her ran two-legged-free —
No thought of British bricks chucked through her door —
And dived in a clean, limp-straightening sea.

1

Ten years after the sale of his trucking business

The white-haired man,
Sitting on the cage-bird balcony
Of his seventh-floor council flat,
And sipping his routine mug of nescaff,
While the first summer sun
Spreads gold on all the street but him . . .

Another old man might dream
That the coffee was Cretan wine
Reflecting the winks of kerchiefed and bangled hand-clappers
As they beckoned the "you-with-a-glass" to join in a
Sunbronzed cartwheel of bodies through
Empires of wish-fulfilment,
Or dream that the balcony dropped to an
Ultramarine lagoon
Of fishes – purple and golden – in shimmery
Turquoise and silver fronds, where feasting
Would start when they hung the twilight with torches
And called for the shell-rattling necklace-girls
To thump the pale sand with laughter-dancing . . .
Other old men might be able to dream
Pictures on pictures, that coupled, uncoupled
And whirred out of sight like dragonflies
Over a river of reeds and heat-haze
Into a whitening, eye-closing sun . . .
Other old men . . .

But this old man,
His mind calloused by humping account-books,
His hands worn to stumps by clutching steering-wheels,
Thinking himself too fat for action
And therefore too old for dreaming,
Can only reach with his eyes
Into a dim incoherence of young-girl breasts and buttocks,
Then, having finished his coffee, pad
Slowly in floppy slippers back
Inside his blotched wallpaper room,
To switch on the telly and watch
Perfectly breasted models
Diving like tropical fishes
In and out of coral sea Martini-ads,
Without ever realising his inconsolable sadness.

The piano-playing tramp

for Alex

An East-End priest describes one of his regular visitors:

"He appears like a drowned man's ghost,
Dripping the seaweed of bombsite and meths-bottle
With the East End clinging to his scalp like lice,
To sit in our golden church of glass and mosaic
Letting the light trickle through his fingers
Down on the keyboard of piano or organ
Till it liquefies into old-time music.
Our graveyard's Victorian salon-balladeers
Poke their skulls round their tombstones to listen.
One hour later the music ceases.
He shuts the keyboard lid,
Slides back into the pondweed of his anonymity.
The gap of black water that he opened
Closes behind him . . ."

The wood-carving sailor

The old man crouched on the stony ground,
His cupped hands clutching a lump of wood
Marked by the waves like a face with a wound —
A baboon-angel, or a troll-prince toad.

The old man fingered the breaker-chiselled bark
And chuckled deep in his sailor eyes:
"There are many crooked secrets" he said "that lurk
In a figurehead carved for you by the seas . . ."

And, just for a moment, the squatting boy —
Who called on the old man half for a laugh,
Bringing cheese or a hunk of bacon pie —
Saw the old man's world with the covers off,

Travelled back with him past seventy years
Of monsters embedded in his clawed face,
Through the atoms of the driftwood, to sail by the stars
Of a dying man's nuclear universe.

The case of the sunrise spraygunner

Alfred Edward Jenkins, 53, widower, of 17 Khartoum Gardens, Upper Tooting, charged with having entered as a trespasser a building known as 13, Fishponds Villas (owned by Percival George Blenkinsop, 37, civil servant, unmarried), doing unlawful damage to the said building by defacing one wall of the front room with a so-called abstract mural painting, asked for nineteen similar offences to be taken into consideration.

With slivers of metal and wafers of plastic
He slid through burglar-proof front doors,
Laid out his rainbow range of spray-guns,
And squirted sunrise on the facing wall.

Purple, orange, vermilion, magenta,
In cloudy streaks with flashes of blue,
Tropical dawns ripened like mangoes
On the walls of tax-inspectors' front rooms.

Arrested. "Case of the Sunrise Spraygunner."
The defence: "I'm giving my light for free,
So rush-hour traffic's home-coming drabness
Will open on morning by a tropical sea."

Fined. Costs. One month in prison.
Paint-rollers wipe his butterfly skies
With uniform beige, cream, candytuft,
Or that pale grey called Brilliant White.

Fifty years after the sunlight-spreader's
Suicide candle burnt down to its end,
One unwiped sunrise-house in Tooting
Was declared a National Monument.

Surbiton Harry

Harry rushes out of his house, dreaming of dolly birds, but catches sight of himself in a shop window and ends up by buying a hot-dog.

Surbiton Harry's randy brain,
Plum-cake-full of goddess dreams,
Burps dragons frothy with shooting-stars
Over his trellis of runner beans.

Rampaging past the dusty laburnums,
He cat-on-the-tiles accosts High Street,
Whose aitch-pee windows of 'Up-Yours, Joneses'
Sneer "Harry, you need a new three-piece suite",

And his gold and scarlet ejaculating
Etna-Vesuvius-tomcat dragon
Shrinks in seven unnoticed seconds
To the texture and size of a plastic-pack banger.

Surbiton Harry's dragon dream
To mount and mate the immortal stars
Sizzles away to a hot-dog munch
That greasily tightens its knot on his heart.

"Three piece suite" is cockney slang for an obvious bit of male anatomy.

Chocolate-box blonde

"Some people" she said "are like chocolate bars –
To be snapped and eaten in small pieces.
Others are more like mintoes or fruit drops
To be sucked slowly till they disappear.
But all of them – whether their centres are hard
Or soft – melt when licked.
                              I like people.
I have people every day after dinner."

Miss Elsie Fitchett,
who keeps herself to herself

"I live at eighty-seven Oak Drive;
But the only oak grows in my garden.
It was planted six hundred years ago
When all of this town was pathless forest
With wolves and bears, archer-robbers,
And squint-eyed magicians chanting spells.
I praise the chance that saved my tree
Under whose shade so many have . . died . . .
Whenever the Australians in ninety-one
Throw a party round their new pool
And keep me awake with their singing and cork-pops,
I wander out in my nightie and slippers,
Stretch my body against the trunk,
And will: – that the stabbings my oak-tree has witnessed
Touch the hearts of the rowdiest Australians . . .

Several neighbours who gave noisy parties
Have died recently . . ."
                              murmured Elsie Fitchett.

The hole

For three hours every morning
Hunched against the cold
In several dirty sweaters
He crouched beside the hole.

Slowly the clammy darkness
Greyed to the drabness of dawn.
In the painful warming of sunrise
He stretched on the awkward stone.

Then, as the light rose higher,
Showing details of twig and leaf,
He shuffled home to his cottage
And another day with his grief.

"Have you ever seen the creatures
Which you think live in the hole?"
"Never," he answered gruffly.
The village called him a fool.

But he knew from the depth of his failure
That the act of staring at void
Was the nearest his desperation
Would ever come to joy.

A man with dandruff in a tube-train smiling to himself: Sonnet

Some glittering fancy minces through his brain,
Plucks peacock feathers from star-spangled air,
Hangs rainbows from his undistinguished hair
And tugs him – like a child with daisy-chain –
Away from briefcase pasties, away from under
Balance-sheet clouds in stomach-ulcer skies,
As, for a moment, his parched mudflat eyes
Flood with a far monsoon, whose tiger thunder
Only he in his dandruff suit can hear.
Is it some Cleopatra on some Nile,
Ready to crown him as her Anthony?
Is it that God has whispered in his ear?
Is it some masterpiece of man's folly?
We shall not know, but may applaud his smile.

Flop

In a bucket of black water
Was reflected a star.
"Stars are enormous, lad,
And ever so far."

While the boy was watching,
Their donkey called Flop
Stuck his head in the bucket of water
And drank every drop.

"Dad, what marvellous creatures
Little donkeys are.
Flop's belly is extra-terrestrial.
It can swallow a star."

Paradise Lost, according to Jimmy Rootback

In *The Goat and Grapes* last Friday evening
Jimmy Rootback said:
"That Adam-an'-Eve business —
Know what I'd 'a done —
If I'd 'a bin Adam, that is?
Out with me axe. Down with the apple-tree,
'Fore it could do any mischief."

Canterbury Bell love-song

The sky was as blue as a Canterbury Bell.
Then wham! Crash! Wallop!
Explosion! There you were,
Brushing against my face,
Like a rose-petal, like a fritillary butterfly.
I tumbled backwards. My blood solidified,
My veins becoming thin rods of rusty salt.

Now I am melting the strings of my piano,
Fusing seven-octaves-worth of music
Into a splodge of copper —
Such white-hot currents are boiling out of my fingertips.

If you dare to settle on my hand,
I shall run wild with delight,
Vault naked onto the banqueting table
And dance through the Mayor and Aldermens' dinner
In honour of the Sewage Disposal Board
Till their ears are so full of the compost of music
That papayas, those magical melons,
Sprout from the dirt in their fingernails.

If I am never
To float with you, froth-light
In the hushed whispers of moonrise,
I shall go rapidly mad in the minutest detail,
With my legs and arms becoming four sides of a box
Which will shut me into the square of the circle.

Blow-dry

Watch out!
I've discovered a way to stream my molecules
And transport myself through space.

For instance, now, at this moment,
As you cuddle, naked and lazily warm from your bath,
To blush yourself pink by your fire,
And monster-like, closer and closer,
Comes the phallic hot breath of your hair-drier,
Watch out!
I've adapted the hair-drier switch,
So that the on-position
Beams my molecules into its jet
To play through your damp, blowing hair,
Run like infinite fingers over your strokable skin,
Nestle into your secret places,
And there do unmentionable things
Which will make you squeal with pleasure.

So remember, love, from tonight,
Whenever you switch on the drier —
Watch out!

This message is more than a load of hot air.

The two lovers on separate sides of an impending civil war

Politicians are vomiting the wine
Which we pressed out with our kissing lips.
Communiqués bomb the nave of our minds
As we're lighting candles in our love's crypt.

They've stuffed our sunlight in a small steel box
While they infest our walls with screams
Which will snuff our candle love and dock
The waving tails of our scampering dreams.

For their foulest destruction is that the hate,
Which will scorch the fruit and vines from our hills,
Will kick us – yes, us – kick us apart
Into separate armies taking aim to kill.

Nootka princess

Come to me, come, silent woman,
From the wild, white water.
Soft foot, hazy lips,
Furred in the sea otter.
Stroke my skin with sleepiness
While the dream-folk heap on us
Blazing embers, hotter, hotter . . .
And the wolf-man at your side
Dissolves in bitter laughter.

14

Island love-song

Pine-covered ridges edge into a sea
Which is foam-covered purple sucking white sand.
Orange lichen warms grey crags.
Cicadas tittle our ears asleep.

Slithering shimmers of unheard sound —
Our bare feet on pine-needle carpet.
Your brown skin's luminous darkness
Floats on me, resinous; humped beasts growl,

Somersaulting our bodies onto a shore
Devoured by white-backed rollers, which break
For ever, for ever, for ever, till space-
time, stretched like a goatskin on furrier's board,
Is tugged by our loving to a new shape.

Upside-down song

Tonight we'll be drinking the air
Which spills from the sea
As we float upside-down
On our gallop across
The moon-and-candlelit universe
Of your gold hair,
With canyons and crags and bits of the earth flying free
Into meteorite-glittering space, while the mincing frowns,
Ink-stained gowns
And pince-nez of logic are cardhouse-tumbled, for prayer,
Kisses and dance to take charge of this evening, when we
Aloft on this moment here, reign everywhere.

15

The teddy-bear cobras

This evening the cobras are friendly.
They nuzzle our faces like spaniels.
Oh, their ominous presence glitters
With the incandescence of their death-dealing numen.
But tonight, for tonight only,
With us they will play teddy-bear.
For tonight, in your dark presence,
The jagged silhouettes of the grinders,
Waiting, clenching their multi-jointed robot arms,
Waiting to jerk me away from your harvest tenderness,
Have been changed by the force of this anti-nightmare
To the arms of mere picture-spotlights
On the walls of a concrete room, which tonight
Is no longer a snakepit of dreams,
But a bower made velvet by the scent of your shadow.
So tonight, for tonight only,
Let the warm tongues of teddy-bear snakes glide over us,
As we melt in the buttery fragrance of your low laughter.

At the deathbed of the nun who broke her vows

Reverend Mother speaks:

"She used to sit so still —
An ikon's within-light
Inking the air around her.
Once, broken vows had crowned her
Sensual rebellious will
With Aphrodite's treacherous grace —
Our Rule's disgrace.
But now that passion-sweating month of summer moonlight
Has long ago been killed
By years of frozen vigil, till
The chilly fingers of endless peace
Can drop on her scrapped nun-body
Another finished tapestry
Of neatly woven suffering,
Another web of criss-
cross lines over a face
That fought, then fought itself,
Then snapped itself as the bread of the offering."

Lake-lady

Murmur of water, buzz of bees,
Shimmer of branches in a frail wind
Lifting pink blossom off the trees —
The tresses of summer becoming unpinned —

She floats like skipping thistledown.
Our eyes, our hearts knock. Now her drum
Thumps through the dull streets of our town,
Throbbing in whispers: "Come, come, come,

"Follow my humming bees downstream
Through a playful haze of petalled scent,
Walk on my lake adaze with dreams —
And drown there for my merriment."

The green god's touch

Fairer than lily, fairer than rose,
The maiden was perfume of summer dawn,
Breeze on the wings of a butterfly.
Naked she lay on the dewy lawn

To breathe the source of nature's power,
To absorb in her flesh the spirit of life.
She stretched her muscles, opened her lungs,
Offered herself to growth as a wife.

Power surrounded the place where she slept.
The green god touched her earth with his kiss.
That night, growing through her body, seeds,
Tree-tall in an hour, ripped her to bits.

Light from a stone

for Eileen

"We were drifting" she'd say "on what
Can cocoon a person's nature in light,
Then hatch it into such dazzling flight
That human becomes what human was not.

"I was scattered through this man's flesh
To the most distant balance-point
Of the last universe, then joined,
Cell by cell, cell by cell, afresh.

"Once he had been smashed out of time
By that crass breaking-up of bone,
Better to reflect light from his stone
Than risk kisses which might ooze slime."

And so she kept her slowly wrinkling
Face free from touch of coarse male hand,
Chained by an unforged wedding band
To a star which, when she died, did not stop twinkling.

After Wordsworth's
"I travelled among unknown men"

"Oh I've done the Katmandu bit.
Sat around smellin' enough lamas' and maharishis' dirty feet
To last me a lifetime.
Now I'm back in a pad dahn Wappin' 'Igh Street,
And it's great, man, great.

"All that bells-an'-incense, it's a bad trip, man.
I was real sick.
You can stuff your falafels and peppermint tea
Up your mustapha.
What I could use now – cod and double chips
Wiv a pickled gherkin.

"Maybe it's dahn to a matter of birds.
So what if I screwed myself silly
Wiv Brahmins and yashmaks and spaced-out Yanks –
The only girl I could ever face marryin'
Is that Lil who worked for Jacob's bike-shop.

"I tell you, up them 'Imalayas
Wiv the snow and them yetis
Makin' footprints over me big as man-'oles,
All I could fink of was comin' 'ome,
And walkin' Lil dahn the Isle o' Dogs.

"Now I'm 'ere on the Isle o' Dogs.
But Lil's gorn.
And it's like I wanna go dahn wiv my face in the gutter
And kiss the soddin' pavement
'Cos she once stood there."

Imitation of Fitzgerald's *Rubaiyat*

Time snuffles up to us on slippered feet,
Spectacled, cardiganed, drab but discreet.
He moves so slowly, it seems he does not move,
Covering furniture with his dust-sheet.

He moves so slowly, whistling through his teeth,
And slowly the bright carpet underneath
His quavering steps blossoms with dingy mould
Which serves us all as universal wreath.

Oh love be true – but, whether true or not,
Time will spread mildew from one tiny spot
Across the fruit-bloom of your lip-loved skin.
For when time kisses us, our brains will rot.

The first portrait

written after seeing an exhibition of ice-age art. The exhibition included one thumb-sized carving of a man's head which has so much detail in it that it must be a portrait. The figure was found in Dolni Věstovice, Moravia, Czechoslovakia; its date is 25–26,000 B.C. I now discover that I remembered it incorrectly as carved from reindeer antler. Though most of the carvings from that site are antler, this one was done in mammoth ivory. Ivory or antler, it is a remarkable head. It seems almost incredible that a sculptor of so long ago could create such a sense of character.

"Carving shadows reach out of the fire
And drag the bones of your face to the surface,
As I scrape and gouge this reindeer horn,
Till a twig the size of my thumb tells me:
'Yes, I will be his head, his nose,
The jut of his jaw, the set of his eyes –
His face to watch as he watches himself
In the dark, still water before the ice
Smudges the pool.'
                 Wait, lord, Huge silence
Struck at me then:–
               the spiky god
Who fastens the white spear leaves on trees
When the green leaves have browned and fallen,
Who tugs the hunter's hair from his head
And withers or knots his running muscles,
The spiky god is prickling the skin
Of my neck, and trying to paint me pictures
On the eyes at the back of my head. Such pictures:–
My thumbhead of reindeer horn in the hands
Of strange, soft people with peeled skin
Wearing strange, thin furs that are also hairless,
In huts as huge as a hill with walls
Of air, and hundreds of suns inside them.
God tells me a thousand lives have passed,
A thousand generations have died,
Since you and I huddled into this hut
To cut off the claws of the stalking ice
With little knives of orange flame,
And transform this twig from the head of a deer
Into your dear head, my lord and master.

Now, over this picture the ice-god is squeezing
A taste, like the muddy foretaste of thaw,
Pain-taste of blood returning to cramped
And frozen limbs – pain which is joy
At the running to come. But the pain and the joy
And the pictures themselves are bounding away
Like reindeer in flight. The pool smudges over . . .

The twig of horn lies here in my hands
Transformed to your face, and that, without
Hairless people, or walls of air
With hundreds of suns hanging down from a roof –
Your face like a twig in my hand is miracle enough for me."

Thumbnail song

for Tony, who, when we came across this head at the exhibition of
ice-age art, made the remark quoted.

Oh yes. We must return again,
Again, again, to the grave grace
Of this aeon-old thumbnail face
Carved on a scrap of antler when

The human world was chinks and cracks
In almost universal ice.
This face once lived, gave wise advice
In some great council, then fell back

Into ice-age oblivion.
If his spirit now reappears,
It is simply to tell us: "Here,
And everywhere, all men are one."

My thanks to Miss Penny Robinson of **The British Museum** *for supplying*
information about this head.

The tree of second sight

The tree with the gift of second sight
Grows on a hill hidden from the town:
Its flowers — the eyes of an innocent bride;
Its trunk — a king who has just been crowned.

Those who are granted to sleep in its roots
Will speak the language of fish and bees,
Will wear the mystic's jumping-shoes,
Then, strolling down river, will be suddenly seized

By the unseen hands, hurried away
To the place of wisdom, and taught such truth
That all who hear them will take what they say
And pelt them with it like rotten fruit.

When I am king

for Hugh Maycock

When I am king,
I'll wear a robe of autumn gold
And deep blue sky,
And tell my fierce red subjects: "Hold
Up your rich dying. Do not die.
I am your king."
But they'll reply:
"Such robes are only won by dying."

I held the song in my hands

I held the song in my hands
Like a scarlet and golden bird,
Like an ancient, painted vase.
But my hands were forced apart.
The bird flew out of sight.
The vase fell and shattered.
It was only then that they told me:
"We are ready to hear the song,"
As they turned their heads away
To discuss in echoing whispers
The question of additional taxes.
A deaf-mute slave swept up
The vase's painted fragments.
I could not even snatch
The piece with the face of the girl,
As my bird with a hundred others
Was served on a silver dish —
Third course of the banquet
For the tax-discussing councillors.

Old age make-up

The actor in his dressing-room:

"Nightly I sit for a couple of hours
Watching the face in my mirror age:
Putty puffing and flabbing my cheeks,
Patched and blotched thready blood-vessel
Bags and wrinkles thumbed into the putty;
Stuffing to pad my stomach and arse;
Wig to dissolve my curly red hair
Into grey wisps on a nude skin dome.
I drop the spectacles on my rheumy nose,
Attach the cord of my hearing-aid,
And shuffle, stick-propped, out to the lights
To carn my salary for the presentation
Of nature's vilest obscenity — age.

"Three hours later I watch for my face,
Pallid with spirits and cleaning-oils,
To emerge from the blotches and skin-sag.
                                    Each night
I try to give thanks for the miracle
Which throws away my stick, my specs,
My hearing-aid at the curtain call,
Remembering the millions of innocent clowns,
Who, like the mask-swapping mime with the wrong
Mask stuck to his terrified face, are trapped
With old age puttied on their skin for keeps."

Death of a dancer

for . . .

At the time of the gift-giving
He was granted toes that could balance on falling leaves,
Legs that could leap from one feather to another
In a downrush of storm.
When it was him to lead the dance
We became smoke-petals, hovering over volcano-mouths
With the zzzheeeeip of spears quivering into the target.
Now he is gone —
Blown off the edge of his cliff,
Feather which sank like a knife as it touched the ocean.
We who are left behind can only
Stamp and howl and stamp,
Stamp with our calloused feet on a patch of earth
Which is now no more to us than a split drumskin.

Test result

We look at you, shifting our feet.
Whatever you do we'll be embarrassed.
Whether you seem tetchy and harassed,
Or whether you're still polite and sweet.

We wonder if you should be eating and drinking
Normal meals. Can you have whisky?
Are you on a diet? . . .Have a . . water-biscuit . . .?
If only we knew what you are thinking.

Have you been told? Haven't you guessed?
D'you find our behaviour this evening odd?
I want to shout: "You poor old sod,
It's positive — your cancer test."

Now, only the fire can tell

Now, only the fire can tell
What the tree might have said
To the man who shaped it into a bed
Where he and his lover experienced Hell.

Industrial accident

The press squeezed tight.
Hand mangled till the bone
Crushed.
One finger dangling. Flesh
And grease and cardboard mushed
With blood seeping.
The steel squealing.
The squealing man.
Weeping.
Broken.

At home, brocades, veneers and vinyl.
His wife? Entertaining,
While the kids are sleeping.

The night-shift shuffles home, shocked, shaken.

Next morning
New safety regulations posted.

The man sneaks out of hospital half-masted,
Shamed by the stump of boredom yawning
Where the five sprinters ran:
Stump, unproductive, final . . .

Unovertime-earning man.

Holiday death

*On the death in Holiday, Florida, of a woman aged forty-three, who,
while having her appendix out at the age of six, went into a coma in which
she remained for thirty-seven years without once regaining consciousness.*

Today Death gloats
Over no athlete's muscle-taut body
Snagged and jagg'd by hammering stab-wounds,
Over no chess-champion brains
Slopped by bullets against a wall,
Over no boat of life-saving heroes
Chewed to fishmeal by lightning-streaked waves,
Over no poison, no bomb,
No screaming fall from tower or cliff-ledge.
Today Death gloats
Over his slowest, gentlest easing
Of human being to fertiliser
Through nearly forty years of sleep.
A child, a six-year old child, for whom
Schooldays, the first vibrations of womanhood —
Giggling-time, swooning-time, kissing-time —
And sex and marriage and child-rearing and work,
All, all have been spent in sleep.
Now, today,
When her daughter's child, had there been a daughter,
Might have already celebrated her sixth birthday,
Now, today,
After so many years
Of growth and muscle change,
Of swelling breasts and menstrual blood,
Then slumping waist and wrinkling skin,
And a few whitening hairs,
Not once seen in a mirror,
Not once accompanied by a single word or gesture,

Now, today,
After so many years
Through which the movements of life
Were movements made by others –
Those professional watchers,
Body-wipers and turners,
Implanters of plastic in veins –
Now, today,
Some force within her has risen
To sickle the sleeping-beauty forests hedging her coma
And touch her almost frozen lips.
But this
Prince Charming kiss
Does not undo her eyes
For her to recognise
Her husband, and, though somewhat old, to start
Living and loving and being loved,
But
Imperceptibly,
Inexplicably,
Chooses this moment to put
A final stop to her heart.

Attempted escape

The engine coughed, spluttered, stopped.
Snowdrifts. Potholes. A gale of a night.
Six shivering people. Distant shots.
"We have to walk now. Come on. Try,"

Said the man with large ears who lifted the torch
And brandished himself like light on the road,
Helping the selfish old woman to walk,
Making himself a screen from the snow.

He strode ahead. He became their eyes.
He kept them warm by telling bad jokes,
Till out of the darkness – a shot at the light,
And the blood of the leader poured black on the snow.

Murder by hypnosis

"This trick, this trick," said the hypnotist
"This trick will be my last."
Silence floated the length of the hall
Like a bat's wings made of glass.

He spread the air with peacefulness
Like honey on crusty brown bread.
The audience relaxed with carefree smiles . . .
And slept themselves to death.

No reprieve

Tomorrow, at dawn, they will come
In masked solemnity.
They will say: "I'm afraid it's time,"
And avoid looking at me.

They will lead me out to a wall,
Tie a blindfold over my eyes.
Priest, gov'nor, and a warder or so
Will mutter a few lies.

Then, as the clock strikes eight,
On the crack of a ten-pound whip
Blood will spurt from my head
And put me to sleep.

Now I know I am cursed,
For tonight I should be seeing
The secret of the universe,
The mystery of being.

Now, at the end, I witness
No vision of Heaven and Hell,
No proof I'm immortal spirit —
Only my blank-walled cell.

Mystic or schizophrenic

To the bone-sharp prophet,
Honed to a hunting-knife with fasting,
There were as many kinds of silence
As there were animals:
Slow, long-necked silences like giraffe-heads
High in the leaves;
Galloping panic silences like hoof-drumming wildebeeste;
Burrowing dung-beetle silences.
Each beast-silence spoke to him in its own language,
Bringing all creatures to his small cell,
Until one day a leopard silence
Neckbone-snapped him into non-existence.

Filling our bodies with space

Filling our bodies with space
Our lungs with light
Till we toss the mountains over our backs
Though every cataract
Becomes a mirror in which we see
Our doppelgänger's face
Displaying the lesson of ecstasy's flight
That body must be stripped of flesh
For the hollow nowhere which is left
To be set free.

In the consulting room

"This morning" he said "at a quarter to twelve precisely,
I saw the workings of my brain:
Bands of dull gold, like melting bookshelves,
Shifting imprecisely over and under each other,
Fading to blackness. Then, in the distance,
A circle of small red blocks,
Like asteroids whirling in space,
Each a regular, oblong,
Shiny, metal, brick.
But every brick was botched," he said,
Clutching with nail-white joint-cracking fingers at the table,
"And I was being sucked into space
Through my own brick asteroids
Into blacked-out vacancy."

The doctor, who seemed to be taking notes
With enormous care,
Was doodling pictures of tree-stumps
And writing his wife a shopping-list.

When the patient had finished his tortured oration
Of inner space-war bombardment,
The doctor raised his head,
Looked the patient full in the eyes for eleven seconds,
Then mumbled into another pad,
While scribbling a prescription for Valium.

Breakdown story

The storm
Wriggles into my ears like maggots,
Champing my mind's connections,
Then spitting them out to form thin galaxies
Of streaky stars.
The storm
Naturally shatters windows,
Topples cupboards,
Tips over concrete floors like tugging a tablecloth,
But in my house-head only.
Outside, the maggot teeth
Disdain to pulp people.
Outside,
They simply say:
"Poor chap, he's going mad."

Suicide at a board meeting in a hotel room

As the table
Reared like a mad horse
Kicking senior executive faces
In all directions like mud clods,

As the walls
Began to chatter excitedly
Of secretary-tupping heart-attacks they had witnessed,

As the carpet
Writhed and twisted to ulcer-serpents
Chewing the intestines of the senior accountant,
Then gliding away, cobra-hooded,
Through a mane-bristling, hoof-hacking jungle,

The reprimanded salesman,
Demanding air,
Shoulder-shrugging the lack of a balcony,
Stepped through the window,
And . .
           for a few seconds . .
                              flew . . .

Massage for back-pain treated as a yoga exercise

for Lutchman Naidoo

He stretches his fingers and presses my spine,
Fingertip-walks on my back like hooves
Of a tiny eohippus which climbs
From my marshy hollows to my world's roof,

And gallops ridges, volcano rims
In month-day-long Icelandic dawns,
Where grey-green gods have named me prince
And lord of the mountains, the desert, the storms.

The fingertips pause. Hands huge as oaks
Lever open my back like a castle wall
Crashed and crushed at the ram's third stroke.
Invaders jostle, push through the hole.

Then in the breached gap, which is all that is left
Of me, the conquering army revels.
A good king reigns. From east to west,
From north to south, his bright peace travels.

Down from a mist-wiped mountain the daughter
Of a singing shepherd walks to the city,
Searching for me under God's orders.
We meet. We dance until we are giddy.

At the moment we touch in our first kiss,
The giant hands click me back – healed.
Shepherd-girl, castle, are lost in the mist . . .

Such mist-loss longing is health's woe-weal.

*I have allowed myself a touch of poetic licence: eohippus, the horse's
ancestor, a creature the size of a fox, did not have hooves.*

Peace the conqueror: Vilanelle

In utter stillness may our storms of fear,
Suspicion, hate, greed, pride, ambition, lust,
Quite overcome, name peace the conqueror here

Where we can feel the lodestar centre near
Us, drawing us to its magnetic trust
In utter stillness. May our storms of fear

Now have their chance to rage so loud and clear
Through our stunned souls, that we collapse, concussed,
Quite overcome. Name peace. The conqueror here

Has to hang trembling on the cliffs of sheer
Panic, and, as he does, welcome each gust
In utter stillness: "May our storms of fear

Join with your storms of mockery to jeer
At our best work, swamp us with mouldy dust.
Quite overcome, name?" Peace, the conqueror, here

Gladly obliterates each separate tear
Of rage or pride, each "I've done", each "I must".
In utter stillness may our storms of fear,
Quite overcome, name peace the conqueror here.

Acceptable print

"Right," they said. "You ready now?
Not that it makes no difference.
It's your turn, mate — no swapping places."
They grabbed my arms and legs,
Laid me out on a marble block
And connected the electrical contacts.
Over my stretched body
Was a flat, black rectangle,
Roughly eight feet by four,
With various glass windows, some instrument dials
And several cables attached.
The one who had spoken took readings
With what looked a bit like a light-meter
On different points of my body — feet,
Knees, groin, midriff and forehead.
He gave a signal. Someone threw a switch.
The block descended slowly. My life
Ran like a speeded-up movie through my consciousness.
"Acceptable print" one of them muttered.
"Photographically fine. Sound undistorted."
Tone of voice for routine quality-check.
That was the last thing I knew. The block descended,
Crushing me flat — rolling me out
As a strip of celluloid. Then a rapid rewind
Round a spool fixed to one end of the block.
A projector switched on. They ran the film
At double speed. "Fine. That'll do."
They rolled me off on another spool,
Dropped me into a can already labelled with my name,
And marked: "For the attention of the Angel of Judgement."

The defocussing process

Faces in jagged alleys
Blank as footballs
Hard as limestone —
We are washed past
As if by a torrent of water,
Eyes blurring from speed and spume.
But this is no water.
Only the creaking of drought and drought-warped surfaces.
This speed is also illusion.
We are still passing that one, motionless face,
Moon-white, parched and dusty . . .
We? But where are the others?
"Correct, sir. You've guessed at last."
A voice of toneless plastic.
"You have now entered the defocussing process.
Your time is more or less . . .
Up . . ."

Many are called, but few are chosen

The crucifix jumps from his cell wall,
Booting his back, tattooing scars
Of the kind of shame that the nails of tarts
Might scratch on their trick in a flophouse brawl.

Fasting, he tortures himself with prayer.
The crucifix, opening empty eyes,
Wafts him near heaven, then — joke! surprise! —
Pinpricks his balloon, sucks out the air,

Drops him in the dung. He croaks that mud,
Even mud can shine like stars.
He limps after larks. Clanging cage-bars
Close round his heartbeat, clamp his mouth shut.

The nearer he crawls to God in prayer,
The clearer he sees the Creator's face
As the One Who is prepared to waste
Almost all His creation, Who cares

In the end for the chosen survivors, the few
Mature cod left from the million eggs.
He hears the crucifix call: "Reject.
Return this protein to the primal brew."

The sixteenth vision

The sixteenth vision:
"You are a gate. A gate opening.
A gate wrenched open by stampeding animals
As they shove and jostle for the unfenced pasture.
Hooves, horns, tongues, nostrils
Hurrying through you; fur, scales, prickles
Rubbing against you; the thud of gallop,
Pitter-patter of scampering paws, the swish
Of tails; the snorting, panting joy
Of escaped beasts in a free landscape.
Rejoice in their haste, their manifold oddities,
And, above all, in the fact that the only
Way in which *you* impinge on their consciousness
Is the pleasure you give them by failing to function."

The peace-piece joker

"To the man who has peace, all money, power,
Status, possessions, and fame,
Will come to be seen as of no importance."
"But peace never remains."

"Oh yes, peace can remain," he said
"If that is what you desire."
Then he grabbed a lump of jagged rock,
Pinned me by the ears,

Neatly slit the skin of my back
And sewed the rock inside.
"This piece of rock" he guffawed "is your peace.
This load will free your mind

"From every desire for money, power,
Status, possessions and fame.
For nothing whatever will hold your attention
Except for this piece of pain."

The journey is inwards

The journey is inwards, yes:
To a world that is perched on the end
Of a hair from the last bee born
In the summer just gone.
But most who attempt the journey,
Unable to shrink
Their over-developed selves
To antenna-size, are held
As dinosaurs, in the terminus,
Classified as extinct.

No "Heaven-Haven"

The old nun to the novice who thinks that the contemplative life is a life of tranquillity:

"It is a place where silence will stalk
Like tigers over your skin,
Where the furry creatures of purring talk,
The whispers, the welcoming grins,

"That promised you a placid trip
Through hush of cloistered twilight,
Will, on your arrival, be ripped
To offal by tiger silence."

Shadow on the spine

                              In the hall of mirrors
He stripped me, and made me stand
Surrounded by images of my naked back.
Pointing he forced me to watch
The dark shape settle on the small,
And shadow outwards like vulture wings,
Like frog, like toad silhouette.
"Now it has touched you," he said with a smile,
"It will feed and grow and obliterate you.
Think, if you like, of frog, toad, vulture.
But not as monsters. No.
Vulture as cleanser of rotten carrion.
Toad as controller of garden pests.
Frog as leaping fly-destroyer.
Think of yourself as a piece of carcase
To be tidied away by leapers and swoopers.
Wear this black shadow in the pivot of your spine
As if you were carrying a king on your back,
And − for your brief time left − it may teach you to fly."

The pain-gift

"This is my gift, this knot of pain,
To be fastened inside your jumping knees
And displayed like a chafing garter of pearls,
So whenever you leap you remember Me,"

Said the Voice from the dark of the crushing cloud
That squirted pain through the saint on the floor
Who tried to smile as his nerves convulsed,
Tried to gasp – "More, Lord, more –

"But no – if pain may be worn as a garter
Of gold and jewels – that is too great honour.
My body, my mind, will too quickly vomit
Dead insects of pride into Thy pain's honey."

"I know," said the Darkness. "Whatever I give
Risks being fouled by the pus of your greed.
But I wager this pain, whatever your intentions,
Will squeeze you to grapeskin and blow you to Me."

The mystic

1

The cat scorches
The grass towards me
With a rope of flame.

Far, far beneath us
The city of ants
Fails to notice the cat,
Thinking its blackness merely a stormcloud.

But we are part of the blackness,
Hurled far above the city —
Ripped pieces of the cat-fight.

2

Water thuds down like steel
To hammer me out of this body
Into the wrigglings of plankton.

The brain's thin film
Of electrical nerve connexions
And inimitable computations
Extends like algae
Over an infinite ocean.

Now, all that is left
Is for each algae particle —
Each thought, each brainwave —
To be eaten, one at a time, by the fishes.

3

Hundred-handed air
Feels for my spine,
Lifting my sunken, supine body
From the molten floor,

Without wings
Or upward motion,
By the centrifuge
Of space's equilibrium,

While earth peels off
On the normal busyness
Of its twirling axis,

And the speed of equilibrium increases
To disintegration.

4

This disappearing I
Remains.

This I?
Remains,
Disappearing . .

These remains
Disappear . . .

This disappearance
Remains . . . .

These eyes . . . . . ?

Eucharist: Vilanelle

Come, take the chalice, praise the Crucifixion,
Praise this destruction of Him Who is Lord
Of everything. You are, without restriction,

Here offered all the riches of affliction,
All the flicks from each scourge's knotted cord.
Come, take the chalice. Praise. The Crucifixion

Tells you: "Each loss, each slight, each least constriction
On your freedom demands to be adored."
Of everything you are, without restriction,

You must give everything now: self-eviction
Of yourself from life-tenure and life-hoard.
Come, take the chalice. Praise. The Crucifixion

Lurks in each sip of wine like an addiction
For which you strip yourself of bed and board,
Of everything. You are, without restriction,

Freed from your flesh, and, whipped by benediction,
Welcomed to choose this death as your reward.
Come. Take the chalice, praise the crucifixion .
Of everything you are without restriction.

Glorified now, as a numbing reminder
That your journey to heaven was easier than theirs."
The lame saint rejoiced as he watched the prosperous
Being allowed to join the blessed company
Of the crippled, disfigured, malnourished and brainstruck.
He praised God Who has made heaven possible
Even for the rich and beautiful . . . .

The lame saint

In the hallway of heaven the lame saint
Was issued with a pair of golden crutches.
"What's this?" he said. "Reminder of my misery?
They're over-ornate and quite impractical.
Gold will bend under my weight."
"Remember," said the angel, laughing, "you're weightless.
It's the pointlessness of your crutches here
Which consecrates them as triumphal sceptres
For you to bear as your badge of honour.
Nor must you think to escape in heaven
The memento of your earthly disability.
For that was your path to heavenly sanctity.
Because of it you were spared many tests
Other saints had to face. Look over there —

The lame saint

In the hallway of heaven the lame saint
Was issued with a pair of golden crutches.
"What's this?" he said. "Reminder of my misery?
They're over-ornate and quite impractical.
Gold will bend under my weight."
"Remember," said the angel, laughing, "you're weightless.
It's the pointlessness of your crutches here
Which consecrates them as triumphal sceptres
For you to bear as your badge of honour.
Nor must you think to escape in heaven
The memento of your earthly disability.
For that was your path to heavenly sanctity.
Because of it you were spared many tests
Other saints had to face. Look over there —
That tiny group — they were rich and famous,
With whole limbs and healthy bodies — —
Just a few — those few — did achieve sanctity
Against all odds. You must carry your crutches,
Glorified now, as a humbling reminder
That your journey to heaven was easier than theirs."
The lame saint rejoiced as he watched the prosperous
Being allowed to join the blessed company
Of the crippled, disfigured, malnourished and brainstruck.
He praised God Who has made heaven possible
Even for the rich and beautiful . . .

Christmas Eve

Here, where neon fingers play piano-scales up credit-cards,
Where children's laughter is chemical-coated like Sugar Wheaties,
Where ladies in leopardskin coats — oblivious of vulture-beaks
Snipping and tailoring rotten leopard-flesh
To neat, white skeleton-suits laid out on the Kenyan hills —
Stuff the well-capped teeth of their smile
With miniature vulture and leopard claws
As they nibble their neighbours, morsel by morsel, in clouds
Of crumbling meringue for elevenses,
While the smiles they have polished with Colgate and Crest
Float away from their faces
To smother bank-managers and tax-inspectors
In a peppermint sea through which they sail
To the Happy-Ever-After Islands
Of Martini, Coke and Bacardi.
Here in this greenhouse-cum-shrine of our greed
Electronic machines pour out
Paper-tape-from-cash-register
Jangles of Christmas carols,
Whose words, if anyone heard them, would say
That, at a particular moment in history,
God turned Himself to a man, who could
Have chemical-coated Wheaties,
Shot almost extinct leopards,
Sat on sofas mouthing meringues and reputations,

Or strutted with tax-dodging steps
Over stretched-out bodies of sun-oiled models
Posing all over drink-ad tropical islands,
But instead went round in a sacking tunic,
Announcing that people who do
Chemical-coat Wheaties,
Shoot leopards, eat meringues,
Tax-dodge through models on tropical islands —
Not to mention the models themselves,
Who, after all, are "only in it for the money" —
Can, if they choose, become
For all intents and purposes . . gods.

OCCASIONAL VERSE
Soul of a nation

for Bridget

A poem written on commission for the BBC film of that name about the Royal Family of Thailand, first transmitted at a time when it appeared quite likely that Thailand might be invaded by the Communists, and its ancient culture reduced to the same kind of rubble and nothingness as the ancient culture of its neighbour, Cambodia/Campuchea.

The proper name of the city we call Bangkok (in approximate phonetic spelling) is:—
Krungthep Mahanakhon Bovorn Ratanakosin Mahintharayuthaya Mahadilokpop Noparatratchathani Burirom Udomratchanivet Mahasathan Amornpiman Avatarnsathit Sakkathattiya Visnukarmpradit

which translates:—
Great City of Angels, Supreme Repository for the Divine Jewels, Great Land Unconquerable, Grand and Prominent Realm, Royal and Delightful Capital City, Full of the Nine Noble Gems, Highest Royal Dwelling and Grand Palace, Divine Shelter and Living-place of the Reincarnated Spirits

Great city of angels,
Supreme repository for the divine jewels,
Mystic east pinnacle-glitter
Fairy-tale fantastical
Child-myths whirled round our heads in profusion
Like genies whooshed out of bottles,
We come and gawp at you,
Great land unconquerable,
While the world's magic countries,
Which once sprouted stories
For children to plunge their faces in
Like mouths into peaches,
Are one by one flattened
To the mindless dust of political slogans,
Tank-track-crushed by huge grey pamphlets,

Here you proclaim yourself —
However illogically,
However rashly —
Great land unconquerable,
Grand and prominent realm,
Royal and delightful capital city,
Full of the nine noble gems,
Not only that sparkling river-bed
Litter dropped by the ages —
Ruby, diamond, emerald,
Topaz, garnet, sapphire —
But the nine gems of blessing,
Purity, wisdom and peace.
Highest royal dwelling and grand palace,
Where one of the last of the world's kings,
Consecrated, set aside by anointment,
Set aside to lead a people by serving them,
Continues to reign,
Divine shelter and living-place of the reincarnated spirits,
Where the past is alive in the present,
The present is part of the past,
And where both present and past
Welcome the angels.

Poet Bloodknot

for Cosmo

May we tonight not talk of Sharpeville:
Of mad laws pulling people out of their earth —
Wild flowers to be dumped and wither on roadsides;
Of the vicious little bits of paper that chased you
Like rabid dogs away from those
White-housed grape-lined valleys, where we
Should now be sitting and getting drunk
On the best Libertas in Stellenbosch.
May we tonight for a moment forget
The teachers, actors and poets whom cops
With saracen steel-plate skins have shown
The view from penthouse window-sills
And taught the game of "Let's pretend
To be blackbirds, ja! . . ."

May we not talk of war, of mad
Broederbond bombers breaking the back
Of every zebra in the Kruger Park,
Every gardener and cook in Soweto,
To build with their bones a radioactive laager
That will keep out the men whose great-great-grandmothers
Their great-great-grandfathers married.
                                        There are
Too many things we had better not mention
If tonight is to be a jolly celebration.
Not even the moment of our first meeting,
When out of a dither of English literati
Running Oxbridge fingers through publicschool hair
At their Yoruba guests who've "kicked in the only —
Needless to say uninsured — talking-drum"
And various Nigerian poets chasing
Other guys' women, you emerged,
Dressed in traditional African drummer-boy
Silvery blue to recite with almost
Impossible innocence the pilgrim poem —
'Lost in Mother Idoto's legend' —
As you looked, if not up at heaven, then at least
At the craning lens of my telly camera,
Displaying your cheek-bones with film-star proficiency.

56

But we may not even talk of that meeting:
Our fizz with the new African poetry –
Soyinka's Ogun: Okigbo's Orpheus –
Such talk would lead too quickly to the war –
That preference by motorists of Britain and France
For the massacre of Biafrans over riding bikes –
Which snatched both poets from discussing Orpheus
And slashed their bloodknot: Okigbo shot
In error by his own soldier; Soyinka
Locked in his two-year chiming silence
Of solitary confinement.

War can rip even poet bloodknots;
And war is reaching for our part of Africa.

No, tonight Annette and I are here
To wish you joy as U.S. citizen.
We hope you forgive us for all the abuse
We've hurled at you on various disreputable
London stages, for being out of step,
Or missing your harmony – not to mention
Forgetting your lines, or arriving at tea-time
For a morning rehearsal!
                         Hamba kahle, Cosmo.

If we need a South African image to end with,
What more appropriate than the Voortrekker monument?
Let's use that obscenity for its proper purpose –
A mould to make a Moir jelly
For all the children of Africa, while we
And any other poets who care to join us
Sit on top with the whole of Chateau Libertas
To drink as we conduct the children
In the number, Cosmo, for which, in spite
Of your vast knowledge of African literature,
You are most famous among your friends –
The song of the Volga boatmen!

Epilogue to a Diverting Spectacle

Such is the wit of Mackintosh and West,
Aided by Robertson, that from his rest
The ghost of Garrick rose, and, nearer Spain
By some nine furlongs, rebuilt Drury Lane
Inside a playhouse called the Ancient Vic —
Spectacle to make envious Barry sick,
Old Cibber jibber, and Quinn quake with rage,
All three reduced to bit-parts on his stage.
Oh what a feast of phrase, of scorn, of banter!
(And what was in that freely poured decanter?)
How many epigrams did there parade!
How many were the worthies well portrayed:
Hopkins, the shuffling prompter, and the stout
Johnson that West played turn and turn about;
Beauties aplenty, gowned in costly style,
Each greeting us with a more radiant smile
Than milkmaids from Jove's own celestial dairy,
Each brought to life by the divine Miss Carey.
What joy it was to see our Hardiman,
Warbling like a seductive waterman,
Forsake his wartime role of chasing airmen —
Save for a paragraph of plosive German.
And oh the music! No coloratura's runs
Could be soprano-er than Sullivan's,
While forte-piano tone forever lingers
In any ear caressed by Burnett's fingers.
But above all the Stratford earth is quaking;
Poor Shakespeare's ghost is shivering and shaking,
Fearful lest Garrick, now back from the dead,
Think to rewrite all that Will ever said:
Consumptive deaths for Rosalind and Celia,
Lear living, Edgar married to Cordelia,
And six fine babes to Hamlet and Ophelia.
For here on the Vic stage is Garrick's stance
To very life, each gesture, tone and glance
Captured by such deft Richardsonisation
That here's no acting but *Reincarnation.*

Written for a Prospect Theatre Company evening at the Old Vic to celebrate the two hundredth anniversary of Garrick's death with a biographical programme selected from writings of the time by Iain Mackintosh and directed by Toby Robertson. Richard Burnett was at the forte-piano; Ian Richardson played Garrick, with the other characters being played by Timothy West, Jan Carey, Hugh Sullivan, and Terence Hardiman who was at that time best known for his role as a Luftwaffe officer in a TV wartime escape series *Secret Army*.

I am unfair to Garrick for his rewrites of Shakespeare. He was notably better than his contemporaries — it was Nahum Tate who gave *King Lear* its happy ending. But Garrick, mercilessly cutting *Hamlet*, Act V, referred to "all the rubbish of the fifth act", and, having slashed *The Winter's Tale* into a three-acter which he called *Florizel and Perdita*, wrote this presumptuous prologue:

> "Lest, then, this precious liquor run to waste
> 'Tis now confin'd and bottled for your taste,
> 'Tis my chief wish, my joy, my only plan
> To lose no drop of that immortal man."

Poet Bloodknot

Cosmo Pieterse, poet, actor and editor from the Cape, a "Coloured" according to the classifications of apartheid, has been a stateless exile since his departure from South Africa on an Exit Permit in the 1960's. I wrote this poem for a joint performance we gave at the National Poetry Centre in London on September 10th, 1981, when we thought that Cosmo was leaving for a university job in the U.S.A. with the prospect of American citizenship. However, bureaucracy intervened again, and he is still stateless.

Sharpeville, an African township in the Transvaal, was, on March 21st, 1960, the scene of a peaceful demonstration against the pass laws, at which the police fired on the crowd, killing 63 and wounding 191. The name has strong symbolic overtones for South Africans.

Chateau Libertas, the name chosen for its ironic connotations, is one of the great Cape vineyards.

Stellenbosch, an enchanting old Cape Dutch town, has the major Afrikaner university.

Saracen — an armoured car.

Broederbond — the Afrikaner freemasonry.

Wole Soyinka, a Yoruba, was imprisoned for protesting against the Biafran war. The central section of his book on his solitary confinement is called *Chimes of Silence. Ogun* is the chief Yoruba god, with characteristics analogous to those of both Zeus and Odin.

Christopher Okigbo, the Ibo poet, wrote his major poem on the Orpheus myth in an African setting; from this comes the line quoted.

It is a South African joke that the *Voortrekker monument,* an ugly piece of fascist-looking architecture, resembles a *Moir* jelly-mould.

Hamba kahle is Zulu for "Fare well; fare forward."

What the Critics have said about Leo Aylen

On *Greek Tragedy and the Modern World*

'This very young sage writes with an impressive authority about the issues which
matter most to all of us.'   *Philip Toynbee, Observer*

On *Discontinued Design*

'Leo Aylen is a pop poet, one of the few whose work looks interesting on the page.
Read or sung aloud his stomping rhythms and often ingenious repetitions must be
very effective indeed.'   *Julian Symons, Punch*

On *I, Odysseus*

'Mr Aylen is a learned poet . . . Explosively floral.'
Derek Stanford, Books and Bookmen

'Classical in origin, dramatic in form and extreme, even apocalyptic, in imagery.'
Geoff Page, Canberra Times

On *Sunflower*

'Feeling, indignant, compassionate, he can sum up a state of mind as well as any
novelist. He knows how humanity ticks.'   *Joan Forman, Eastern Daily Press*

'I regard Leo Aylen as being a poet unusually competent and unusually sincere. The
competence is a part of his mastery of classical poetry and his skill in translating it;
the sincerity is his own attitude to life today, concentrated into words that really say
what they mean.'
John Bayley, Wharton Professor in English Literature, Oxford University

On *Return to Zululand*

'Leo Aylen is an accomplished poet. His imagery is tough and earthy, his observations
of apartheid telling. An extraordinary book of portraits.'
Michelene Wandor, Time Out

'Clarity and a compelling narrative shape that seizes the reader's attention.'
Shirley Toulson, British Book News

'A good collection this.'   *Thomas McCarthy, The Irish Times*

On *Red Alert: this is a god warning*

'The imaginative strength of the poetry is outstanding. His intellectualism is balanced
by a Zorba-like vitality and a fine perception.'   *Gordon Strachan, BBC Radio 4*

'His poem is taut, alert, deliberate, owes much to the daily tensions of dallying with
death.'   *Ann Nugent, The Stage*

As Poet-Performer

'At its best, live poetry reading is like super-condensed, intense theatre and Leo
Aylen's offering was like a mini drama festival in itself. He writes in such a way that
readers of his printed work must hear in them some of his intended pace and accent.
But his own rendition is almost perfect, utilising all the genre has to offer in word
music, cadence, speed and aural kaleidoscope. His acting was superb.'
Elaine Durbach, The Argus

'An entire TV programme devoted to poet Leo Aylen was still not enough for me.'
Val Pauquet, The Star

'He achieves genuine pathos with his poem *Poor Old Jones*, gently satirises
bureaucracy, and his scathing attack on South African apartheid froze the audience.'
Graham Donaldson, The Scotsman

On his film *Dynamo*

'It was technically brilliant, exuberantly sincere, marvellously entertaining.'
Anthony Burgess, The Listener